I0448165

February 2013

REGISTERED SEX OFFENDERS

Sharing More Information Will Enable Federal Agencies to Improve Notifications of Sex Offenders' International Travel

GAO

Accountability ★ Integrity ★ Reliability

GAO-13-200

GAO
Accountability * Integrity * Reliability

Highlights

Highlights of GAO-13-200, a report to congressional requesters

REGISTERED SEX OFFENDERS

Sharing More Information Will Enable Federal Agencies to Improve Notifications of Sex Offenders' International Travel

Why GAO Did This Study

In recent years, certain individuals who had been convicted of a sex offense in the United States have traveled overseas and committed offenses against children. GAO was asked to review what relevant federal agencies—including DOJ, DHS, and the Department of State—are doing with regard to registered sex offenders traveling or living abroad. This report addresses the following questions: (1) How and to what extent does the federal government determine whether registered sex offenders are leaving or returning to the United States? (2) How and to what extent have federal agencies notified foreign officials about registered sex offenders traveling internationally? GAO analyzed August and September 2012 data from the U.S. Marshals, USNCB, and ICE on registered sex offenders who traveled internationally. GAO also interviewed relevant agency officials and surveyed officials from all 50 states, 5 territories, and the District of Columbia to determine the extent to which they identify and use information on traveling sex offenders.

What GAO Recommends

GAO recommends that ICE consider receiving the automated notifications and DOJ and DHS take steps to ensure that USNCB and ICE (1) have information on the same number of traveling registered sex offenders and (2) have access to the same level of detail about each traveling registered sex offender. USNCB within DOJ and DHS concurred with our recommendations.

View GAO-13-200. For more information, contact Eileen R. Larence at (202) 512-6510 or larencee@gao.gov.

What GAO Found

Three federal agencies—U.S. Marshals, International Criminal Police Organization (INTERPOL) Washington – U.S. National Central Bureau (USNCB), and U.S. Immigration and Customs Enforcement (ICE)—use information from state, local, territorial, and tribal jurisdictions, as well as passenger data from the U.S. Customs and Border Protection (CBP), to identify registered sex offenders traveling outside of the United States. Similarly, these agencies may be notified of registered sex offenders traveling to the United States through several means, including tips from foreign officials or when CBP queries the registered sex offender's biographic information at a port of entry and finds that the offender has a criminal history. However, none of these sources provides complete or comprehensive information on registered sex offenders leaving or returning to the United States. For example, CBP does not routinely query individuals who leave the United States by commercial bus, private vessel, private vehicle, or by foot, in which case CBP may not be able to determine if any of these individuals are registered sex offenders. In addition, foreign officials do not always monitor when a registered sex offender is returning to the United States. The Federal Bureau of Investigation (FBI), working with other agencies, is developing a process that will address some of these limitations. Specifically, the FBI will send an automated notice to the U.S. Marshals and law enforcement officials in the jurisdictions where the sex offender is registered that the offender is traveling, to the extent that the offender's biographical information is queried at the port of entry. However, because ICE has not requested to receive the automated notifications, ICE will not be notified of registered sex offenders who leave the country via a land port of entry whose biographical information is queried.

USNCB and ICE have notified foreign officials of some registered sex offenders leaving and returning to the country, but could increase the number and content of these notifications. USNCB notifies its foreign INTERPOL counterparts about registered sex offenders traveling internationally, and ICE notifies its foreign law enforcement counterparts about traveling sex offenders who had committed an offense against a child. USNCB provides more detailed information than ICE because USNCB uses offenders' self-reported travel information that some jurisdictions collect, which may include details such as hotel information. Since ICE uses passenger data, it does not have these details. Also, data from August 1 to September 30, 2012, showed that the two agencies had significant differences in the number of offenders they identified in notifications. USNCB sent notifications on 105 traveling sex offenders that ICE did not, and, conversely, ICE sent notifications on 100 traveling sex offenders that USNCB did not. In part this is because the two agencies rely on different information sources and do not share information with one another. Taking steps to ensure that these agencies have all available information on the same registered sex offenders traveling internationally could help ensure that the agencies are providing more comprehensive information to their foreign counterparts to help inform public safety decisions.

_____ United States Government Accountability Office

Contents

Figures

Abbreviations

APB	Advisory Policy Board
APIS	Advance Passenger Information System
CA	Bureau of Consular Affairs
CBP	U.S. Customs and Border Protection
DHS	Department of Homeland Security
DOD	Department of Defense
DOJ	Department of Justice
DS	Bureau of Diplomatic Security
FBI	Federal Bureau of Investigation
IAFIS	Integrated Automated Fingerprint Identification System
ICE	U.S. Immigration and Customs Enforcement
INTERPOL	International Criminal Police Organization
IWG	International Tracking of Sex Offenders Working Group
MPS	Metropolitan Police Service
NCIC	National Crime Information Center
NSOR	National Sex Offender Registry
NSOTC	National Sex Offender Targeting Center
NTC	CBP National Targeting Center
PNR	Passenger Name Record
SMART Office	Office of Sex Offender Sentencing, Monitoring, Apprehending, Registering, and Tracking
SOCA	Serious Organised Crime Agency
SORNA	Sex Offender Registration and Notification Act of 2006
U.K.	United Kingdom
USNCB	INTERPOL Washington - U.S. National Central Bureau

United States Government Accountability Office
Washington, DC 20548

February 14, 2013

The Honorable F. James Sensenbrenner, Jr.
Chairman
The Honorable Robert C. Scott
Ranking Member
Subcommittee on Crime, Terrorism, Homeland Security, and
Investigations
Committee on the Judiciary
House of Representatives

The Honorable Christopher H. Smith
Chairman, Subcommittee on Africa, Global Health, Global Human Rights,
and International Organizations
Committee on Foreign Affairs
House of Representatives

In recent years, certain individuals who had previously been convicted of
a sex offense in the United States subsequently traveled overseas and
committed an offense against a child or attempted to transport a child
from overseas to commit a sex crime. For example, in 2008, an individual
with a prior U.S. sex offense conviction received a prison sentence for
engaging in illicit sexual activity with a 15-year-old girl in Ciudad Juarez,
Chihuahua, Mexico, in exchange for money and crack cocaine. Also, in
2009, an individual who had previously been convicted of a sex offense
against a minor in the United States was convicted of a child sex tourism
crime, where the individual sexually abused a minor while traveling
abroad.[1]

Given the risk that some individuals previously convicted of a sex offense
may pose, in July 2006, Congress passed and the President signed the
Sex Offender Registration and Notification Act of 2006 (SORNA), which
provided a new set of sex offender registration and notification standards,
including criminal penalties for those who fail to comply with these
standards.[2] These standards require convicted sex offenders to register

---

[1]For the purpose of this report, a child sex tourist is an individual who travels to another
country for the purpose of engaging in illicit sexual activity with a child.

[2]Pub. L. No. 109-248, tit. I, 120 Stat. 587, 590-611.

and keep the registration current in the state, territorial, or tribal jurisdictions in which they live, work, and attend school, and for initial registration purposes only, the jurisdiction in which they were convicted. Registration generally entails convicted sex offenders appearing in person to provide the jurisdiction with personal information, such as name and date of birth, among other information. Jurisdictions then use this information to track these offenders following their release into the community in an effort to ensure public safety. Further, SORNA directs the Attorney General, in consultation with the Secretary of State and the Secretary of Homeland Security, to establish a system for informing domestic jurisdictions about persons entering the United States who are required to register under SORNA.[3] The act also made it a federal crime for a sex offender to travel in foreign commerce and knowingly fail to register or update a registration.[4] Moreover, the Department of Justice (DOJ) promulgated guidelines governing implementation of SORNA that have resulted in some jurisdictions' requiring sex offenders to inform local and state officials in the jurisdictions where they reside of their plans to travel internationally.[5] You requested that we review what relevant federal agencies—including DOJ, the Department of Homeland Security (DHS), and the Department of State (State)—are doing with regard to sex offenders who were convicted and subsequently registered in the United States and who are traveling or living abroad.[6] Specifically, this report addresses the following questions:

(1) How and to what extent does the federal government determine whether registered sex offenders are leaving or returning to the United States?

(2) How and to what extent have federal agencies notified foreign officials about registered sex offenders traveling internationally?

---

[3]42 U.S.C. §16928.

[4]18 U.S.C. § 2250(a).

[5]*Supplemental Guidelines for Sex Offender Registration and Notification*, 76 Fed. Reg. 1630 (Jan 11, 2011).

[6]For the purpose of this report, we only included U.S. persons (i.e., U.S. citizens or lawful permanent residents) and foreign nationals who were registered as sex offenders in the United States at the time of their travel outside of or back to the United States. We did not include U.S. persons or foreign nationals who are not already registered as sex offenders in the United States, such as those who committed sex offenses abroad and may have to register under SORNA upon their return to the United States.

To address both objectives, we identified relevant legislation, regulations, and other guidance that directs federal agencies' efforts to identify registered sex offenders leaving or returning to the United States. We also obtained documentation and testimonial evidence from members of the International Tracking of Sex Offenders Working Group (IWG), which is composed of representatives from various agencies within DOJ, DHS, State, and the Department of Defense (DOD) and was tasked with developing mechanisms for identifying registered sex offenders leaving and returning to the country.[7] We also interviewed agency officials from three of the federal departments represented on the IWG. The agencies within DOJ include the Office of Sex Offender Sentencing, Monitoring, Apprehending, Registering, and Tracking (SMART Office); Federal Bureau of Investigation (FBI); United States Marshals Service (U.S. Marshals); and International Criminal Police Organization (INTERPOL) Washington - United States National Central Bureau (USNCB). The agencies within DHS include U.S. Customs and Border Protection (CBP) and U.S. Immigration and Customs Enforcement (ICE). The agencies within State include the Bureau of Consular Affairs and Bureau of Diplomatic Security.

We also interviewed and surveyed relevant state, local, and territorial officials to determine what role, if any, they play in informing the federal government of registered sex offenders leaving the country, and how, if at all they become aware of registered sex offenders returning to the country, and how they use that information to help ensure public safety. We first conducted a screening survey of officials the SMART Office identified as being responsible for implementing SORNA in each of the jurisdictions—the 50 states, 5 U.S. territories, and the District of Columbia.[8] These officials included representatives of state police departments or attorney general offices. Subsequently, of those jurisdictions that responded that they require sex offenders to provide advance notice of international travel, we selected 4 jurisdictions—

---

[7]DOD was excluded from our review because, under SORNA, the departments responsible for dealing with registered sex offenders traveling abroad were identified as DOJ, DHS, and State.

[8]The 5 U.S. territories included in our review are American Samoa, Commonwealth of the Northern Mariana Islands, Guam, Puerto Rico, and the U.S. Virgin Islands. We did not include federally recognized Indian tribes eligible under SORNA because we will analyze tribal jurisdictions' efforts to implement SORNA and identify registered sex offenders leaving and returning to the United States in a separate review.

Maryland, Florida, Michigan, and Arizona—to conduct site visits and 1 jurisdiction (New Mexico) to conduct telephone interviews. [9] During the site visits, we obtained additional information on how jurisdictions implemented and enforced the requirement and shared information on traveling registered sex offenders with relevant federal agencies. We chose these jurisdictions to achieve variation in (1) the extent of international travel from the jurisdiction; (2) percentage of the population that is composed of sex offenders; and (3) whether the state has land and sea ports of entry, in addition to airports, to cover the various modes by which sex offenders could enter and leave the country. [10] During the site visits, we met with officials from the following federal, state, and local law enforcement agencies: U.S. Marshals, ICE, and CBP (at air, land, and sea ports of entry); state agencies responsible for maintaining the state sex offender registry; and local law enforcement agencies responsible for registering and monitoring sex offenders. While the perspectives from the officials we interviewed during site visits cannot be generalized to all jurisdictions, they provided valuable insights about registered sex offenders traveling internationally.

We also developed and administered a second survey of the same officials from the 56 jurisdictions to obtain more detailed information on the extent to which jurisdictions require registered sex offenders to provide advance notice of international travel and inform federal agencies of registered sex offenders leaving the country. The survey also included questions related to jurisdictions' perspectives on any challenges or improvements needed regarding receiving or providing information about sex offenders leaving or returning to the United States, in addition to other

---

[9]During our site visit to Arizona, the Arizona agency officials responsible for sex offender registration clarified that the State of Arizona does not require sex offenders to provide advance notice of their international travel unless the sex offenders are planning to permanently reside abroad. Consequently, to maintain consistency with our selection criteria, we selected the next state jurisdiction that matched our selection criteria for site visits—New Mexico. State officials in New Mexico did not respond to our request to meet with them; however, we were able to conduct telephone interviews with relevant CBP and U.S. Marshals officials in this state.

[10]Ports of entry—including air, sea, and land ports of entry—are government-designated locations where CBP inspects persons and goods to determine whether they may be lawfully admitted or entered into the country.

issues related to the implementation of SORNA. We received responses from 52 out of 56 jurisdictions.[11]

Additionally, we obtained and analyzed data from the U.S. Marshals, ICE, and USNCB, which are the three agencies identified as having responsibility for taking action based on the information they obtain on registered sex offenders leaving or returning to the country to help ensure public safety. We obtained and analyzed data the three agencies received from August 1 through September 30, 2012 on registered sex offenders traveling internationally.[12] We also analyzed the data to determine the extent to which there was any fragmentation (i.e., circumstances in which more than one federal agency is involved in the same broad area of national interest) or duplication (i.e., two or more agencies or programs are engaged in the same activities or provide the same services to the same beneficiaries) with regard to notices sent to foreign officials. We also assessed whether there were any benefits or drawbacks to any fragmentation or duplication. We assessed the reliability of the data the agencies provided by questioning knowledgeable agency officials and reviewing the data for obvious errors and anomalies. We determined that the data were sufficiently reliable for our purposes.

Moreover, we contacted federal and foreign officials in select countries—Australia, Canada, Mexico, the Philippines, Thailand, and the United Kingdom—to obtain information on how they learn of registered sex offenders traveling from the United States to those countries; how, if at all, they use this information to help ensure public safety; and any limitations or benefits of receiving this information. We selected Mexico, the Philippines, and Thailand because, on the basis of data we obtained from ICE, these are among the countries most frequented by child sex

---

[11]We did not receive survey responses from the following jurisdictions: American Samoa, New Hampshire, Oregon, and Washington. For further details on the web survey, see GAO, *Sex Offender Registration and Notification Act: Jurisdictions Face Challenges to Implementing the Act, and Stakeholders Report Positive and Negative Effects,* GAO-13-211 (Washington, D.C.: Feb. 7, 2013), and for the e-supplement containing the questions and results of the web survey see GAO, *Sex Offender Registration: Survey of States and Territories on Implementation of the Sex Offender Registration and Notification Act (GAO-13-234SP, February 2013), an E-supplement to* GAO-13-211 (Washington, D.C.: Feb. 7, 2013).

[12]We chose this time period because we wanted to assess the effectiveness of a process the U.S. Marshals instituted in August 2012 for sharing information with USNCB on registered sex offenders traveling outside of the United States.

tourists. We selected Australia, Canada, and the United Kingdom because they are known to have national sex offender registries, similar to those of the United States, and have expressed an interest in receiving information from the U.S. government on sex offenders traveling there. Appendix I provides additional detail on our objectives, scope, and methodology.

We conducted this performance audit from January 2012 to February 2013 in accordance with generally accepted government auditing standards. Those standards require that we plan and perform the audit to obtain sufficient, appropriate evidence to provide a reasonable basis for our analysis based on our audit objectives. We believe that the evidence obtained provides a reasonable basis for our analysis based on our audit objectives.

Background

Sex Offender Registration Requirement

The purpose of SORNA is to protect the public from sex offenders and offenders against children by providing a comprehensive set of sex offender registration and notification standards. These standards require convicted sex offenders, prior to their release from imprisonment or within 3 days of their sentencing if the sentence does not involve imprisonment, to register and keep the registration current in the jurisdictions in which they live, work, and attend school, and for initial registration purposes only, the jurisdiction in which they were convicted. Registration generally entails the offender appearing in person at a local law enforcement agency and the agency collecting information such as name, address, Social Security number, and physical description of the offender, among other items. The registration agency also is to document, among other items, the text of the provision of law defining the criminal offense for which the offender is registered; the criminal history of the offender, including dates of all arrests and convictions; and any other information the Attorney General requires. In addition, implementing jurisdictions are to maintain a jurisdiction-wide sex offender registry and adopt registration requirements that are at least as strict as those SORNA established. The length of time that convicted sex offenders must continue to update their registration is life, 25 years, or 15 years, depending on the seriousness of the crimes for which they were convicted and with possible reductions for maintaining a clean record. The frequency with which sex offenders must update or verify their information—either quarterly, semiannually, or annually—also depends on the seriousness of the crime. Once sex offenders register or update their registration in their jurisdictions, under the act, implementing jurisdictions are to provide the new information to FBI's National Sex Offender Registry (NSOR). NSOR is a national database within the FBI's National Crime Information Center (NCIC) that federal, state, local, territorial, and tribal law enforcement officials can access to obtain information on registered sex offenders throughout the United States. Jurisdictions' receipt of certain federal grant funds is conditioned upon whether they have "substantially implemented" SORNA, and, as we have previously reported, jurisdictions are in various stages of implementing the act.[13]

Federal Requirements for Registered Sex Offenders Traveling Internationally

Pursuant to the Attorney General's authority to interpret and implement SORNA, the SMART Office developed SORNA guidelines specifically related to registered sex offenders traveling internationally.[14] For example, under DOJ's National Guidelines, each jurisdiction in which a sex offender is registered as a resident is instructed to require the sex offender to inform the jurisdiction if the sex offender intends to commence residence, employment, or school attendance outside of the United States.[15] The jurisdiction needs to then (1) notify all other jurisdictions in which the offender is required to register through immediate electronic forwarding of the sex offender's registration information, and (2) notify the U.S. Marshals—the primary federal agency responsible for investigating sex offender registration violations under SORNA—and update the sex offender's registration information in the national databases pursuant to the procedures under SORNA § 121(b)(1). Also, under DOJ's Supplemental Guidelines, jurisdictions are directed to have sex offenders report international travel 21 days in advance of such travel and submit information concerning such travel to the appropriate federal agencies and databases.[16] Furthermore, per the SMART Office's SORNA Implementation Document, in order to provide the most helpful information to U.S. Marshals and other law enforcement agencies, DOJ's

---

[13]For a description of requirements jurisdictions must meet in order to "substantially implement" SORNA, and the extent to which jurisdictions have meet these requirements, see GAO-13-211.

[14]42 U.S.C. §§ 16912(b), 16914(a)(7).

[15]The National Guidelines for Sex Offender Registration and Notification, 73 Fed. Reg. 38,030 (July 2, 2008).

[16]See 76 Fed. Reg. at 1637.

guidelines require jurisdictions to collect passport information in addition to other travel information, such as itinerary details, purpose of travel, criminal records, and contact information within the destination country, regarding a registered sex offender's intended international travel.[17] Currently, according to officials from the SMART Office, DOJ will not reduce grant funds for jurisdictions that have not yet implemented the supplemental guidelines on registered sex offenders traveling internationally, because DOJ is allowing jurisdictions additional time to implement the supplemental guidelines as part of its assessment of whether jurisdictions have "substantially implemented" SORNA.

Federal Agencies That Play a Role in Identifying Registered Sex Offenders Traveling Internationally

Under SORNA, the responsibility for establishing a system for informing jurisdictions about persons entering the United States who are required to register is divided among three federal departments— DHS, DOJ, and State—with DOJ being the lead agency. Additionally, in 2008, the SMART Office created the IWG, which consists of multiple agencies within DOJ, DHS, and State, to discuss issues related to identifying registered sex offenders traveling internationally.[18] Although not required to do so under SORNA, ICE's Homeland Security Investigations (HSI) division, consistent with its objective to target transnational sexual exploitation of children, developed the Angel Watch program. The purpose of this program is to provide advance notice to foreign officials when a registered sex offender who committed a crime against a child is traveling from the United States to a foreign country. Table 1 describes the functions of the federal agencies that play a role in identifying registered sex offenders traveling internationally.

[17]DOJ, *SORNA Implementation Document* (Washington D.C.: Mar. 27, 2012). This document is the SMART Office's most recent guidance related to registered sex offenders traveling internationally. It directs jurisdictions to collect passport information from sex offenders prior to their international travel, among other things.

[18]Although SORNA requires DOJ, in consultation with DHS and State, to establish a system to inform domestic jurisdictions about persons entering the United States who are required to register under SORNA, the IWG adopted the expanded language provided in DOJ's National Guidelines for Sex Offender Registration and Notification on sex offenders traveling internationally. The guidelines aimed to establish a mechanism to inform jurisdictions about sex offenders leaving the country in order to effectively carry out the SORNA requirement, since such offenders will be required to resume registration if they later return to the United States.

Table 1: Functions of the Federal Agencies that Play a Role in Identifying Traveling Registered Sex Offenders

Federal department	Federal agency	General function
DOJ	SMART Office, Office of Justice Programs	Provides guidance and technical assistance to jurisdictions and public and private organizations in activities related to sex offender registration. Maintains the Dru Sjodin National Sex Offender Public Website, which is a national online registry portal that the public can use to access information on registered sex offenders.
	U.S. Marshals	Investigates sex offender registration violations and provides operational support to help state, local, tribal, and territorial law enforcement identify, locate, and prosecute non-compliant sex offenders. Provides assistance to jurisdictions in the identification and location of sex offenders relocated as a result of a major disaster.
	U.S. Marshals National Sex Offender Targeting Center (NSOTC)	Functions as an interagency intelligence and operations center to assist with identifying, investigating, locating, apprehending, and prosecuting non-compliant, unregistered fugitive sex offenders. Assists states, tribes, and territories in enforcing the registration requirements.
	USNCB	As the designated representative to the International Criminal Police Organization (INTERPOL) on behalf of the Attorney General, USNCB facilitates the exchange of information to assist law enforcement agencies in the United States and throughout the world in detecting and deterring international crime (including sex crimes) and terrorism through a network of 190 member countries.
DHS	CBP	Inspects travelers entering the United States at air, land, and sea ports of entry. When travelers (U.S. persons and foreign nationals) enter the country through ports of entry, CBP officers conduct a screening procedure referred to as a primary inspection where officers take steps to ensure that the traveler is in compliance with all U.S. legal requirements. CBP officers process travelers deemed admissible at the primary inspection. Other travelers not readily deemed admissible or requiring additional scrutiny are referred to a secondary inspection for a more in-depth interview by a CBP officer. This inspection involves a closer inspection of travel documents and possessions (which could include determining whether the traveler possesses child pornography), additional questioning, and background checks through law enforcement database systems such as NCIC or TECS, among other things.[a] At the end of the secondary inspection, CBP may release, refuse entry to, or detain the person while CBP further reviews compliance or admissibility.
	NTC	Receives travelers' data such as name, date of birth, and travel information from air carrier or cruise ship companies to (1) provide tactical targeting information aimed at interdicting terrorists, criminals, and prohibited items; and (2) match travelers and goods against known patterns of illicit activity.
	ICE	Investigates sexual exploitation of children, among other responsibilities, and operates the Angel Watch program, which identifies convicted child predators who attempt to travel internationally to countries known as destinations for child sex tourism.
State	Bureau of Consular Affairs (CA)	Issues passports to U.S. citizens, adjudicates visas for foreign nationals, and interprets visa laws and regulations, among others. Determines whether visa should be issued to foreign nationals who have committed crimes of moral turpitude, which could include certain sex offenses.
	Bureau of Diplomatic Security (DS)	Works with foreign police and security organizations to coordinate U.S. law enforcement initiatives and investigations, among others.

Source: GAO analysis based on information provided by federal agencies.

Federal Agencies Collect Information on Traveling Registered Sex Offenders, but the Information Could be More Comprehensive

Three federal agencies—U.S. Marshals, USNCB, and ICE—use information from state, local, territorial, and tribal jurisdictions, as well as passenger data from CBP, to determine whether registered sex offenders are traveling outside of the United States. Similarly, five federal agencies—USNCB, ICE, U.S. Marshals, Consular Affairs, and CBP—may be notified of registered sex offenders traveling to the United States through several means, including tips from foreign officials or when CBP queries the registered sex offender's biographic information at a port of entry and finds that the offender has a criminal history. However, none of these sources provides complete or comprehensive information on registered sex offenders leaving or returning to the United States. For example, because CBP's passenger data are based on information from private or commercial air, commercial vessels, and voluntary reporting from rail and commercial bus lines; and CBP does not routinely query individuals who leave the United States by commercial bus, private vessel, private vehicle, or by foot, it is unable to provide information on all individuals leaving the country. In addition, foreign officials do not always monitor when a registered sex offender is returning to the United States. The FBI is establishing an automated notification process that is expected to address some of these limitations. However, because ICE has not requested to receive the automated notifications, ICE will not be notified of registered sex offenders who leave the country via a land port of entry.

Limitations in the Information Federal Agencies Receive on Registered Sex Offenders Leaving the Country from State and Local Jurisdictions and CBP Passenger Data

Officials from the U.S. Marshals and USNCB said that they use information from state, local, territorial, and tribal jurisdictions, and officials from the U.S. Marshals and ICE said that they use air and sea passenger data from CBP, to determine whether registered sex offenders are traveling internationally, but both mechanisms have limitations.[19]

[19]To a lesser extent, the U.S. Marshals reported using information gathered from ongoing investigations to determine whether a registered sex offender is leaving the United States. Depending on the case, the U.S. Marshals may receive this information from state, local, or territorial law enforcement, or other federal agencies.

Information from Jurisdictions	The information that the U.S. Marshals and USNCB receive from jurisdictions about registered sex offenders traveling internationally is limited, in part because (1) some jurisdictions do not require sex offenders to inform them of international travel and (2) those jurisdictions that do require notice must rely on sex offenders to self-report this information. Consistent with the Attorney General's authority under SORNA to require sex offenders to provide additional information for inclusion in the jurisdiction's registry than what the act requires, DOJ's Supplemental Guidelines added that registered sex offenders must provide jurisdictions 21 days advance notice of any international travel, and jurisdictions are to notify the U.S. Marshals of any registered sex offenders traveling internationally. According to the U.S. Marshals, to support these jurisdictions' efforts to provide more complete and consistent information, in February and March 2012, the SMART Office asked jurisdiction registry officials, and the U.S. Marshals and USNCB asked relevant jurisdictional law enforcement agencies, to submit a Notification of International Travel form to the U.S. Marshals. This form includes the traveler's name, passport number, travel information, criminal record, and contact information in the destination country.

However, not all jurisdictions have elected to implement the DOJ guideline requiring registered sex offenders to provide advance notice of international travel. Specifically, of the 50 jurisdictions that responded to our survey question about advance notice of international travel requirements, 28 reported that they require sex offenders to provide such advance notice, whereas the other 22 do not, primarily because their jurisdiction's laws do not permit them to do so.[20] For example, 1 jurisdiction said that because its statute requires registered sex offenders to notify the registry within 72 hours after international travel, officials are not authorized to collect this information in advance. Moreover, some jurisdictions have difficulty obtaining information on traveling registered sex offenders on a consistent basis because jurisdictions must rely on sex offenders to self-report, and jurisdictions have limited mechanisms in place to enforce the self-reporting requirement. For example, sex offender registry officials in 1 jurisdiction we visited said that they would not know that a registered sex offender failed to self-report international travel

---

[20]According to senior officials from the SMART Office, generally, jurisdictions have had to amend their existing sex offender registration and notification laws to include the 21-day advance notice of international travel. However, some jurisdictions are able to make an administrative decision that will permit them to collect this information.

unless they conducted an address verification operation, which would enable them to determine that the sex offender is traveling. Senior officials from the SMART Office stated that they are pleased that 28 jurisdictions have already implemented the advance notice provision, considering that the guidance for the provision was not released until January 2011. These officials also stated that they continue to provide technical assistance to jurisdictions seeking to implement this provision.

Information from CBP's Review of Passenger Data

Information on registered sex offenders traveling internationally that the U.S. Marshals and ICE obtain from CBP's review of passenger data also has limitations. CBP, as part of DHS, has the mission to secure the United States' borders while facilitating legitimate trade and travel. To help fulfill that mission, CBP established NTC, which, among other things, receives and reviews air and sea passenger data to determine whether persons entering or leaving the country via a commercial airline or cruiseline are on the terrorist watchlist, are wanted, or have a warrant out for their arrest.[21] NTC officials stated that in 2009, they met with the U.S. Marshals to determine how they could support efforts under way at the newly formed NSOTC. NTC agreed to review passenger data to determine whether any persons leaving the country are registered sex offenders. Since then, according to NTC officials, they have provided the U.S. Marshals information, such as name, date of birth, destination, and offense, on all registered sex offenders NTC identifies from passenger data so that the U.S. Marshals can verify that the sex offender did not violate any registration requirements. NTC officials stated that they also use this information to identify registered sex offenders who remain in a foreign country for an extended period of time and return to the United States for short periods of time, because this may be an indication that the individual is circumventing SORNA requirements by falsely reporting their place of residency. NTC provides this information to ICE and U.S. Marshals for possible investigation or other law enforcement action. Figure 1 shows the primary methods by which the U.S. Marshals, ICE,

---

[21]NTC uses passenger data collected from the Passenger Name Record (PNR) and the Advance Passenger Information System (APIS). PNR data are collected when an individual books a flight, for example, from a travel agency or airline. Pursuant to regulations, APIS data are collected and sent by airlines as individuals check in for the flight and no later than the moment the aircraft's doors are closed and secured for the flight (or no later than 30 minutes prior to that moment, if transmitted in batches), and by cruise lines 60 minutes prior to the ship's departure from the United States and, for incoming vessels, at least 24 hours (at least 96 hours for voyages of 96 hours or more) prior to arrival at the U.S. port of entry.

and USNCB receive information on registered sex offenders traveling internationally.

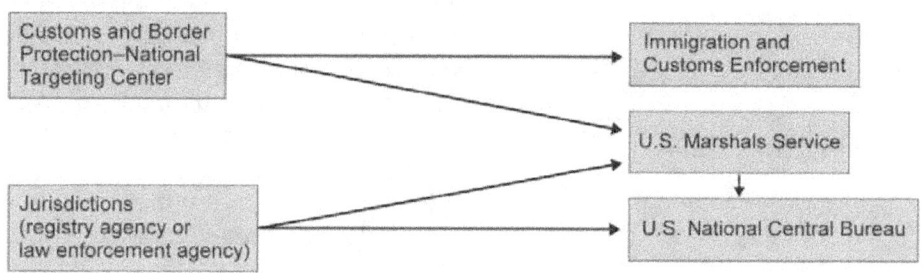

Figure 1: Primary Methods by Which the U.S. Marshals Service, U.S. Immigration and Customs Enforcement and U.S. National Central Bureau Receive Information on Registered Sex Offenders Traveling Internationally

Source: GAO analysis based on information provided by federal agency officials.

While the information NTC provides may be helpful, it has limitations. First, CBP collects and analyzes information on individuals leaving the United States via private or commercial airline, commercial vessel, and voluntary reporting from rail, but does not routinely query individuals who leave the United States by commercial bus line, private vessel, private vehicle, or by foot . Since travelers departing by commercial rail, commercial bus line, private vessel, private vehicle or by foot are not required to report travel information in advance of their travel, CBP may be unable to provide advance targeting and analysis of these individuals. However, a CBP officer may access information on these individuals by querying their biographical information during special outbound operations at port of entry. It is CBP's policy that CBP officers query individuals leaving the country only if there is a special operation underway, such as an operation to verify the amount of currency taken out of the United States.[22] According to NTC officials, CBP officers at the land port of entry are not required to provide NTC with the results of their queries because they are only required to pass information related to

---

[22]Under 31 U.S.C. § 5316, an individual who transports, attempts to transport, or causes to be transported (including by mail or other means) currency or other monetary instruments (e.g. , traveler checks) in an aggregate amount exceeding $10,000 or its foreign equivalent at one time from the United States to any foreign country, or into the United States from any foreign country, must file a report with CBP.

individuals on the terrorist watchlist. Therefore, NTC is generally not able to inform the U.S. Marshals and ICE about registered sex offenders leaving the country through means such as land ports or on a privately chartered boat.

Second, to determine whether a registered sex offender is on a particular flight, NTC determines whether any of the passenger data, such as name and date of birth, match any of the data in the FBI's NCIC. However, NCIC may not always have complete information to enable NTC to determine if there is a match, in part because jurisdictions may enter information incorrectly or not at all because certain fields are not mandatory. In this case, NTC checks electronic public sex offender registries—which are not always up to date—to collect missing information, or calls relevant registry officials—which could take additional time.

Limitations in Information on Registered Sex Offenders Returning to the Country Provided by Foreign Officials and from Reviews of Criminal History Records

Five federal agencies—USNCB, ICE, the U.S. Marshals, Consular Affairs, and CBP— have several mechanisms in place to identify registered sex offenders returning to the United States. For example, USNCB officials stated that their foreign counterparts, to the extent that they are aware, may notify U.S. officials of registered sex offenders returning to the United States. In addition, U.S. Marshals officials stated that they sometimes receive information from NTC on registered sex offenders returning to the United States. According to NTC officials, they are able to provide this information to the U.S. Marshals analyst stationed at NTC to the extent that the sex offender's entire itinerary and flight information are available.[23] However, these mechanisms do not identify all of the registered sex offenders returning to the United States all of the time. For example, even though USNCB may receive information on some returning registered sex offenders through its foreign counterparts, the information these officials provide is based on anonymous tips or offenders' self-reported information. According to USNCB officials, even though hundreds of registered sex offenders traveled outside of the United States from August through September 2012, as we discuss later

[23]In September 2010, a U.S. Marshals analyst was assigned to work at NTC on a part time basis in order to identify potential SORNA violations, such as instances in which a registered sex offender is in violation of his or her registration requirements through international travel without proper notification. The U.S. Marshals analyst began working at NTC on a full time basis starting in June 2012.

in this report, USNCB rarely received notifications of these registered sex offenders returning to the United States.[24] Table 2 describes the mechanisms by which federal agencies become aware of registered sex offenders traveling back to the United States and the limitations of those mechanisms.

Table 2: Mechanisms by Which Federal Agencies Become Aware of Registered Sex Offenders Returning to the United States and Their Limitations

Federal agency	Mechanisms in place to identify U.S.-registered sex offenders	Limitations to the mechanisms in place
U.S. Customs and Border Protection (CBP)	National Targeting Center (NTC) obtains the sex offender's full flight itinerary, including the return trip, if available, prior to when the sex offender leaves the United States.	Not all sex offenders may have booked their return trip in advance.
	Receives an alert that the traveler has a National Crime Information Center (NCIC) record when CBP officers query traveler's biographic information at air or sea ports of entry.	
U.S. Immigration and Customs Enforcement (ICE)	Receives sex offender's full flight itinerary, including the return trip, if available, from NTC prior to when the sex offender leaves the country.	Not all sex offenders may have booked their return trip in advance.
U.S. Marshals	Receives sex offender's full flight itinerary, including the return trip, if available, from NTC prior to when the sex offender leaves the country.	Limited to those registered sex offenders for whom NTC had returning trip information.
U.S. National Central Bureau (USNCB)	Notified by foreign INTERPOL counterparts.	Limited to anonymous tips or self-reported information INTERPOL counterparts receive.
U.S. Consular Affairs	May identify individuals with an outstanding warrant when reviewing a U.S. citizen's application for a passport renewal or replacement submitted while the person is in another country.	Limited to registered sex offenders who need to renew or replace their passports and have outstanding warrants.
	Notified when consular officers abroad verify criminal records in NCIC of a foreign national who applied for a U.S. visa.	If Consular Affairs grants the visa, the agency is not aware of when the registered sex offender is actually traveling to the United States.

Source: GAO analysis based on information on traveling registered sex offenders that federal agencies provided.

---

[24]According to USNCB officials, USNCB is only able to track registered sex offenders returning to the United States when another INTERPOL counterpart reports that information to USNCB. Otherwise, USNCB does not systematically track when registered sex offenders return to the United States.

An Automated Notification Process Currently Under Development Is Intended to Address Some Challenges with Identifying Registered Sex Offenders Leaving and Returning to the United States

To help ensure that relevant federal agencies are more consistently notified of registered sex offenders leaving or returning to the United States, in 2008, the SMART Office established the IWG.[25] The IWG is charged with developing an international tracking system to identify registered sex offenders leaving and returning to the country and immediately relay this information to appropriate domestic law enforcement agencies for any additional action as needed, such as to initiate an investigation. Specifically, FBI officials stated that, in collaboration with other IWG member agencies, they are developing a process that will send an automated notification to the U.S. Marshals' NSOTC and registry and law enforcement officials in the jurisdictions where the sex offender is registered: (1) when a registered sex offender has purchased an airline or cruise ticket for international travel, (2) 1 week before the registered sex offender is scheduled to travel by commercial air or sea transport, and (3) when a CBP officer queries that person's biographic information at a U.S. port of entry, such as any U.S. airport.[26]

The automated notification, if implemented as intended, will provide the U.S. Marshals and relevant jurisdictions with information on registered sex offenders returning to the United States whose biographic information is queried by CBP officers at air, sea, and land ports of entry, assuming these offenders enter the country legally and their identifying information in NCIC, such as date of birth, is accurate and complete. In addition, FBI officials stated that the automated notification is expected to provide relevant jurisdictions with information on sex offenders registered in their jurisdiction who did not self-report international travel. This will help law enforcement officers to avoid using resources to search for sex offenders who they thought had absconded, when the offender had actually left the country on personal travel.

---

[25]For more details on the federal agencies represented on the IWG, see appendix I.

[26]The automated notification will be sent whenever a registered sex offender engages in travel with a U.S. nexus; that is, entering, transiting through, or exiting a U.S. port of entry by commercial air or sea transport. The system will send notices for registered sex offenders exiting a U.S. port of entry by land or private boat only to the extent that CBP queries these travelers' biographic information. FBI officials responsible for implementing the automated notification stated that a notification will also be triggered if a change is made to the Offender Status Field in NCIC to indicate the offender is traveling or has moved outside of the United States.

According to FBI officials, the FBI vetted the automated notification proposal through its Advisory Policy Board; the FBI Director approved the proposal in June 2012; and FBI officials estimate that they will be able to implement the automated notification as early as March 2013.[27] FBI officials responsible for implementing the automated notification said that they are currently working with CBP to include additional information from CBP's systems in the automated notifications, such as the specific ports of entry and the mode of transportation offenders are using. The FBI will not delay implementation of the automated notification to incorporate the additional information from CBP; instead, the FBI will incorporate this information into the automated notifications at a later date, if necessary.

While the automated notification will address some of the limitations discussed previously, it will not address all of them. For example, according to FBI officials, the automated notification will provide notice to the U.S. Marshals and jurisdictions of all registered sex offenders leaving or returning to the United States for whom CBP officers query their biographic information at a port of entry. Consequently, the automated notification will not provide notice of a registered sex offender who plans to leave the country via a land port of entry because CBP generally does not query information for these travelers. CBP officials explained that CBP officers may query biographic information for individuals leaving the United States through a land port of entry—such as in the case of a special operation to verify the amount of currency taken out of the country—but generally do not do so because of regulatory, policy, and infrastructure limitations in monitoring individuals leaving the United States.[28] Table 3 discusses the extent to which the planned automated notification is intended to address the federal government's current limitations in identifying registered sex offenders traveling internationally.

---

[27]The Advisory Policy Board (APB) is comprised of representatives from federal agencies that participate in the FBI's Criminal Justice Information Services Division programs and tribal and local law enforcement and criminal justice agencies, and it establishes guidelines for systems maintained by FBI's Criminal Justice Information System. APB working groups provide input on systems proposals and recommendations to the FBI Director for implementation.

[28]According to FBI officials responsible for implementing the automated notification, they have had preliminary discussions with Canadian Police Information Center officials as to whether every person that enters Canada through the U.S.-Canada land border will be queried in NCIC.

Table 3: Extent to Which the Planned Automated Notification Is Intended to Address Limitations to Identifying Registered Sex Offenders Traveling Internationally

Limitations to identifying registered sex offenders traveling internationally	Automated notification intended to address limitation?	Efforts to address limitations not addressed by the automated notification
Registered sex offenders leaving the United States		
Some jurisdictions do not collect information on registered sex offenders' international travel, and, therefore, are not able to notify relevant federal agencies.	Yes	
Jurisdictions that do collect information on registered sex offenders' international travel may not receive complete information because they rely on sex offenders to self report or on community members to provide tips about the sex offenders' travel.	Yes	
The U.S. Customs and Border Protection (CBP) does not have a mechanism to routinely query travelers leaving the United States by land ports or private boat in order to determine whether they are registered sex offenders.	No	The Department of Justice's Sex Offender Sentencing, Monitoring, Apprehending, Registering, and Tracking Office (SMART Office) provides technical assistance to jurisdictions seeking to implement the requirement that registered sex offenders provide 21-day advance notice of international travel, including travel by land ports or private boats.
NTC relies on National Crime Information Center (NCIC) data to determine if any traveler leaving the country via a commercial or private airplane or a commercial ship is a registered sex offender; however, some NCIC data may be incorrect or incomplete, thus making it difficult for NTC to determine if there is a match.	No	The automated notification will also rely on NCIC data, and, therefore, may have similar limitations. The International Tracking of Sex Offenders Working Group (IWG) continues to encourage registry officials to enter in a timely and complete manner all of the mandatory and optional information that NCIC will accept.
Registered sex offenders returning to the United States		
The. U.S. National Central Bureau (USNCB) relies on self-reported information offenders provide to foreign law enforcement about returning to the United States.	Yes	
CBP generally does not notify relevant federal or jurisdiction officials of registered sex offenders returning to the United States unless the offender is wanted or has a warrant.	Yes	

Source: GAO analysis based on information on traveling registered sex offenders that federal agencies provided.

The fact that the automated notification will not address all limitations will likely remain for the foreseeable future because they are inherent to well-established processes for entering and exiting the country. For example, according to senior CBP officials responsible for field operations, conducting inspections that would enable them to collect information on all travelers exiting the country via a land port of entry would require policy, regulatory, procedural, and major infrastructure changes.[29]

The automated notification, when operational, is also intended to help ensure jurisdictions are more consistently notified of registered sex offenders returning to the United States, which may enable them to take public safety measures they deem appropriate. Of the 56 sex offender registry officials who responded to our survey questions about the extent to which federal agencies provided notice of registered sex offenders returning to the United States, 17 reported that they received notice of registered sex offenders returning to the United States from at least one federal agency.[30] Federal officials we interviewed identified several reasons why they do not consistently provide this information to sex offender registry officials in the jurisdictions. For example, CBP officers at 3 of the 10 ports of entry stated that it would not be feasible to notify jurisdiction officials of all the registered sex offenders they identified because of the number of travelers returning through their ports of entry.[31] Also, according to USNCB officials, they generally do not notify jurisdiction officials of returning registered sex offenders unless the foreign country provides USNCB with this information. Further, U.S. Marshals officials stated that they share information on returning registered sex offenders with state and local law enforcement agencies if the planned return date of a sex offender leaving the country is known.

---

[29] We have previously reported in GAO, *Overstay Enforcement: Additional Mechanisms for Collecting, Assessing, and Sharing Data Could Strengthen DHS's Efforts but Would Have Costs,* GAO-11-411 (Washington, D.C.: April 15, 2011) that DHS is required to collect information for certain foreign nationals leaving the country but concluded that it could not do so at land ports of entry without incurring a major impact on land facilities.

[30] Of the 17 jurisdictions that reported receiving information on registered sex offenders entering the United States from a federal agency, 10 reported receiving information from the U.S. Marshals and USNCB, respectively; 8 reported receiving it from ICE; and 2 reported receiving it from CBP and State, respectively. Some of the responses reflect jurisdictions receiving information from more than one federal agency.

[31] Of the 3 ports of entry, CBP officers from 1 port of entry also stated that it would be feasible to notify jurisdictions of those registered sex offenders identified at secondary inspection. Of the remaining 7 ports of entry, 3 stated that it would feasible to notify jurisdictions of registered sex offenders returning to the United States, if these offenders are identified at the secondary inspection, and 4 ports of entry did not discuss the feasibility of notifying jurisdictions.

Jurisdictions could possibly use information on registered sex offenders traveling to their jurisdictions from abroad to help them identify the current location of these offenders. For example, officials from one local law enforcement agency we visited stated that receiving such notifications would help officers verify whether the offenders have returned from foreign travel when officers conduct address verifications. In addition, this information would help jurisdictions fulfill their requirements under SORNA to protect the public from sex offenders. Once the automated notification system is operational, jurisdictions that have registered the sex offender and entered a record into NCIC will be notified that an offender has returned to the United States. Having this information will allow these jurisdictions to implement public safety measures more consistently.

ICE Has Not Made Plans to Receive Information from the Automated Notification, a Fact That May Preclude It from Obtaining Information on Some Traveling Sex Offenders

To help ensure that they obtain as complete information as possible regarding registered sex offenders traveling internationally, the U.S. Marshals and ICE will continue to request information from jurisdictions or NTC even after the automated notification is operational. Currently, the U.S. Marshals and ICE do not consistently receive information on registered sex offenders entering or leaving the country via a land port of entry because NTC does not have this information and jurisdictions receive this information only to the extent that sex offenders self-report it. The automated notification will fill this information gap, in part, by sending notices about registered sex offenders entering and leaving the country via a land port of entry, to the extent that CBP queries the biographical information of the offender, in addition to providing notices about registered sex offenders traveling internationally via commercial air and sea transport. Although the automated notification will provide information on a greater number of traveling registered sex offenders than the number that jurisdictions and NTC provide, as shown in table 4, NTC provides more details on a specific traveler than the automated notification. Further, jurisdictions that collect offenders' self reported data may also be able to provide more details. Therefore, according to U.S. Marshals officials, they find it beneficial to continue to receive information from each of these two sources.

Table 4: Type of Information Jurisdictions, NTC, and the Automated Notification Provide or Will Provide on Registered Sex Offenders Traveling Internationally

Type of information provided	Jurisdictions[b]	NTC	Automated notification[c]
Name	●	●	●
Date of birth	●	●	●
Passport number	●	●	○[d]
FBI number[a]	●	●	○[d]
Photograph	●	●	
Criminal history	●	●	
Whether Victim is a Minor	●	●	○[d]
Port of entry through which the offender will leave or enter the country	●	●	●
Full flight itinerary (for round-trip flights, if available)	●	●	
Whether the flight is inbound or outbound	●	●	
Names of travel companions	●	●	
Where the offender will stay while in country (e.g., hotel information)	●		

Source: GAO analysis based on information provided by federal agencies.

[a]The FBI number is a unique identification number assigned to each individual who has a record in the FBI's Integrated Automated Fingerprint Identification System (IAFIS), a nationwide database of fingerprint and criminal history records of individuals who have been arrested.

[b]A jurisdiction may not always provide all types of information.

[c]Additional information from NCIC will be provided to the extent it is available.

[d]This information may be provided to the extent it is available in NCIC.

According to an ICE section chief responsible for the Angel Watch program, ICE has not requested to receive the automated notifications because it prefers to rely on information NTC provides, which meets ICE's specific needs. In particular, an NTC analyst, after identifying a registered sex offender with plans to travel internationally via commercial air or sea transport, conducts further analysis to determine whether the offender committed a crime against a child. This ICE chief stated that ICE does not want information on all types of registered sex offenders, which is what the automated notification would provide, but only on those who have committed crimes against children, in accordance with ICE's mission to investigate the sexual exploitation of children. However, by not requesting to receive the automated notification, ICE will not have information on registered sex offenders who committed offenses against children, left the country via a land port of entry, and had their biographical information queried at the port.[32] According to the FBI, in order to receive the automated notification, ICE would have to submit a request to FBI's Advisory Policy Board; and given that the board meets twice a year, it could take approximately 1 year or more for the board to approve an agency's request to receive alerts from the system. The FBI also explained that the automated notification will not be able to distinguish between traveling registered sex offenders who committed offenses against children and those who committed offenses against adults because the notifications are derived from NCIC data, and the age of the victim is not a required field in this system.[33] Therefore, if ICE were to receive the automated notification, ICE would have to determine on its own whether the offenders leaving the country through a land port of entry committed an offense against a child. However, according to NTC officials, about 90 percent of the registered sex offenders they identified in fiscal year 2012 who planned to travel internationally via commercial air or sea transport had committed offenses against children. We have previously reported that collaborating agencies can look for opportunities to address resource needs by leveraging each others' resources, which could include receiving the automated notification, and obtaining additional benefits that would not be available if they were working separately.[34] By electing not to receive the automated notifications, ICE will not receive information on registered sex offenders traveling to Canada or Mexico via a land port of entry whose biographical information is queried. This is of particular concern considering that, according to ICE, Mexico is one of the countries to which registered sex offenders travel most frequently. If ICE were to receive alerts from the automated notification, we recognize that some effort would be required to determine whether sex offenders leaving the country through a land port of entry committed an offense against a child. However, the level of effort

---

[32]The number of sex offenders who left the country via a land port of entry whose biographical information was queried at the port is unknown because CBP does not routinely track this information.

[33]According to the FBI officials, the requirement for mandatory or optional fields in NCIC is dictated by legislation and the user community through the Criminal Justice Information Services Advisory Process; and thus, it may not be feasible to change the fields in NCIC.

[34]GAO, *Results-Oriented Government: Practices That Can Help Enhance and Sustain Collaboration among Federal Agencies,* GAO-06-15 (Washington, D.C.: Oct. 21, 2005).

required, and whether or not the benefits of the effort would outweigh the cost, cannot be determined at this time.

ICE and USNCB Notify Foreign Officials about Some Registered Sex Offenders Traveling Abroad, but Improved Information Sharing Could Increase the Number and Content of These Notifications

USNCB and ICE inform foreign officials when registered sex offenders are traveling to their countries to enable these officials to take actions that they deem appropriate to ensure public safety. USNCB and ICE notify their own unique counterparts in foreign countries about traveling sex offenders for similar purposes, such as enabling them to make decisions as to whether they will admit sex offenders into their country. In addition USNCB and ICE notify these counterparts for different purposes. For example, ICE counterparts may monitor the whereabouts of sex offenders while they are in the foreign country. USNCB and ICE base such notifications on different information sources; USNCB uses information it receives from the U.S. Marshals and jurisdictions, and ICE uses information it receives from NTC's passenger data reviews as part of ICE's Angel Watch program.[35] However, the U.S. Marshals do not consistently share information with USNCB on traveling sex offenders, and USNCB and ICE do not share the information they receive on traveling sex offenders with each other. As a result, USNCB and ICE were not able to notify their foreign counterparts about a large number of registered sex offenders traveling internationally from August to September 2012, and some of the notifications were not as comprehensive as possible.

USNCB and ICE Notify Their Respective Foreign Counterparts of Registered Sex Offenders Traveling Internationally for Similar as well as Unique Purposes

USNCB notifies its INTERPOL counterparts in other countries about registered sex offenders traveling internationally. Similarly, ICE, through its Angel Watch program, notifies its foreign law enforcement counterparts about sex offenders traveling internationally who had committed an offense against a child. According to USNCB and ICE officials, USNCB and ICE send these notices to different agencies within the foreign countries, but for similar purposes—to enable foreign officials to decide whether they want to admit the registered sex offender into their country or take other public safety measures they deem appropriate. For example, with regard to the United Kingdom, USNCB notifies its

---

[35]U.S. Marshals officials explained that a U.S. Marshals analyst detailed to NTC manually fills out the Notification of International Travel form for each traveling registered sex offender identified by NTC's passenger data reviews, and sends these forms to the U.S. Marshals investigator detailed to USNCB.

INTERPOL counterpart—the United Kingdom National Central Bureau—which is hosted by the Serious Organised Crime Agency (SOCA), a law enforcement body that fights organized crime. SOCA officials then make decisions about how to use this information. They could share it with agencies such as the United Kingdom (U.K.) Border Agency, which is responsible for refusing entry to persons who do not qualify, or the U.K. Metropolitan Police Service (MPS), which interviews registered sex offenders to establish exactly what their plans are while in the United Kingdom and where they will be staying upon entry or if admitted. On the other hand, according to ICE officials, ICE notifies the sex offender unit within the U.K. Metropolitan Police Service as well as the U.K. Border Agency directly through its attachés posted abroad about registered sex offenders traveling to the United Kingdom who committed an offense against a child. Of the six countries included in our review, three generally do not admit registered sex offenders, and in one country, even though it generally admits registered sex offenders, foreign law enforcement officials monitor the activity of the sex offender while in country. For example, ICE Angel Watch program officials reported that in 2012, an ICE attaché notified foreign officials in advance that a registered sex offender was traveling from the United States to their country; and as a result, the foreign officials denied entry to the registered sex offender. Appendix II provides information on registered sex offenders traveling internationally who were refused entry by foreign countries.

USNCB and ICE identified reasons why it is advantageous that they both notify foreign officials of sex offenders traveling internationally. USNCB officials explained that they have been trying to encourage their INTERPOL counterparts to inform them about individuals convicted of sex offenses in their countries who are traveling to the United States. Therefore, it is important for USNCB to provide such notifications if it expects its counterparts to reciprocate. ICE officials explained that it is important for their ICE attachés to inform their foreign law enforcement counterparts about traveling registered sex offenders to assist the counterparts with tracking offenders visiting that country, such as by developing a shared spreadsheet designed to help the country establish its own sex offender registry, and to monitor sex offenders' activities while in that country.

Federal Agencies Do Not Share All Available Information They Have on Traveling Registered Sex Offenders with One Another, thus Limiting the Number and Content of Notifications Sent to Foreign Officials

USNCB provides more comprehensive information on sex offenders' travel plans to its INTERPOL counterparts than ICE provides to its foreign law enforcement counterparts, and the additional information that USNCB has could help support ICE's mission. USNCB bases its notifications on information that it receives from jurisdictions that require registered sex offenders to provide advance notice of international travel, whereas ICE bases its notifications on information it receives from NTC's analysis of commercial air and sea passenger data. As previously discussed, jurisdictions that require advance notice may collect more information on each sex offender's travel plans—such as hotel information—than NTC does.

In addition, neither USNCB nor ICE has provided its foreign counterpart with as many notices of traveling registered sex offenders as it potentially could. Specifically, as shown in figure 2, from August 1 through September 30, 2012, USNCB notified its counterparts of 105 offenders that ICE did not provide to its counterparts. Further, 82 of these 105 notifications (78 percent) were for registered sex offenders who had committed offenses against children. Similarly, ICE notified its counterparts of 100 offenders that USNCB did not provide to its counterparts.

Figure 2: Notifications Sent by U.S. Immigration and Customs Enforcement and U.S. National Central Bureau to Foreign Countries on Registered Sex Offenders Traveling Internationally, August 1, 2012 to September 31, 2012

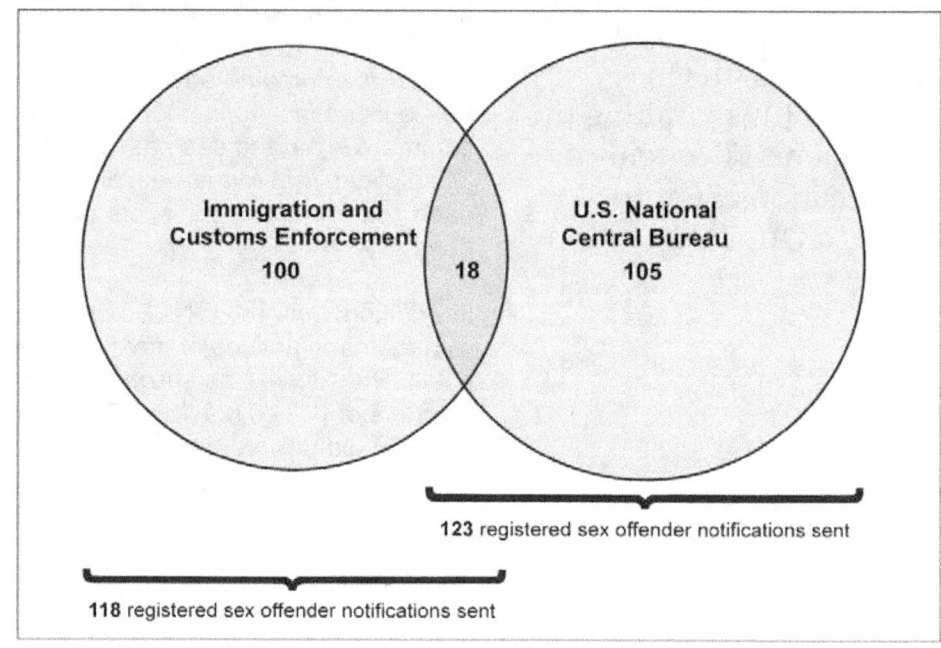

123 registered sex offender notifications sent

118 registered sex offender notifications sent

Source: GAO analysis of Immigration and Customs Enforcement and U.S. National Central Bureau data.

There are several reasons why USNCB and ICE generally do not have information to share on the same sex offenders traveling internationally. First, USNCB generally does not receive information on traveling sex offenders from NTC, whereas ICE does. This is in part because the U.S. Marshals has not passed on all of the information it has obtained from NTC on registered sex offenders to USNCB. We have previously reported that collaborating agencies should consider if participants have full knowledge of the relevant resources in their agency.[36] Consistent with this guidance, in March 2012, the U.S. Marshals assigned one of its investigators to be co-located with USNCB officials in order to provide USNCB with information on sex offenders for whom USNCB would send

---

[36]GAO, *Managing for Results: Key Consideration for Implementing Interagency Collaborative Mechanisms*, GAO-12-1022 (Washington, D.C.: Sept. 27, 2012).

green notices to its foreign INTERPOL counterparts.[37] U.S. Marshals officials then realized that they had additional information on traveling registered sex offenders that could be of interest to USNCB, and starting in August 2012, the U.S. Marshals investigator was to begin providing USNCB information on traveling registered sex offenders that the U.S. Marshals receives from NTC.[38] However, we found that from August through September 2012, the U.S. Marshals only provided USNCB with information on 39 of the 169 traveling sex offenders of whom the U.S. Marshals was aware based on information from NTC.[39]

According to U.S. Marshals officials, the U.S. Marshals analyst posted at NTC may not be informing USNCB about all registered sex offenders traveling internationally that NTC has identified because the analyst's primary purpose is to identify and pursue potential SORNA violations— instances in which a registered sex offender is in violation of registration requirements by traveling internationally without providing advance notice. As a result, by the time the analyst finishes looking into potential SORNA violations, some of the registered sex offenders that NTC identified may have already completed their international travel; the U.S. Marshals investigator posted at USNCB would not notify USNCB about these offenders because the opportunity would have passed for USNCB to provide advance notice to its foreign counterparts about these offenders.

Officials further explained that it takes time to complete the Notification of International Travel form for each traveling sex offender that NTC identifies, which may also prevent the investigator from notifying USNCB prior to the sex offender initiating travel. U.S. Marshals officials also

---

[37]A green notice is one of INTERPOL's system color-coded notices that provide warnings about subjects who may travel internationally and present a possible threat to public safety or to commit a criminal offense based on previous criminal convictions or history.

[38]In particular, the U.S. Marshals analyst posted at NTC is to complete the Notification of International Travel form for registered sex offenders identified by NTC as traveling internationally and send the form to the U.S. Marshals investigator posted at USNCB.

[39]During this same time period, the U.S. Marshals provided USNCB with information that it had received from jurisdictions on an additional 56 traveling sex offenders, and information that it had received from other sources on an additional 4 traveling sex offenders. However, we were not able to assess the extent to which U.S. Marshals provided USNCB with the information it obtained from jurisdictions and other sources because we were not able to obtain the necessary data prior to when this report was to be issued.

stated that they would generally not provide USNCB with information on registered sex offenders whose international travel is less than 3 days. However, USNCB officials stated that they send notifications to their counterparts on all traveling registered sex offenders, regardless of travel duration or ability to provide advance notice.

U.S. Marshals officials explained that they did not receive any additional resources to help bridge the gap between the information that NTC and USNCB obtain on registered sex offenders traveling internationally, but volunteered to help remedy this issue with limited existing resources. While the U.S. Marshals' intentions are commendable, USNCB still does not have access to information on most of the registered sex offenders traveling internationally that NTC identifies, thus precluding USNCB from notifying its foreign counterparts about these individuals and enabling them to make informed public safety decisions.

A second reason why USNCB and ICE do not have information on the same traveling sex offenders could be that USNCB receives information on registered sex offenders traveling internationally from jurisdictions, whereas ICE does not. Third, according to a senior ICE official, ICE may have received information on additional traveling sex offenders, but did not send notifications via Angel Watch because of constrained manpower or insufficient information on the child exploitation conviction, among other things.

According to USNCB officials, they copy several other federal agencies on their notifications to foreign officials, including FBI's Innocent Images National Initiative and the State Department's Bureau of Diplomatic Security (DS) which may choose to take further action.[40] For example, DS officials stated that they share information on registered sex offenders traveling internationally with their regional security officers, who may inform other U.S. government and foreign law enforcement officials in-country, as they deem appropriate. However, USNCB officials reported that they do not coordinate their notifications with ICE, in part because their understanding was that ICE was interested in registered sex offenders traveling internationally only if the offender was the subject of

---

[40]FBI's Innocent Images National Initiative was developed in 1995 because of the increase in the number of investigations that involved sex offenders using computers to share pornographic images of minors. The initiative teams FBI agents and local police in task forces to conduct undercover investigations of suspected offenders.

an ICE investigation; USNCB officials stated that they were not aware that ICE's primary interest in obtaining information on these offenders was to notify their foreign law enforcement counterparts.

We have previously reported that collaborating agencies can look for opportunities to address resource needs by leveraging each others' resources and obtaining additional benefits that would not be available if they were working separately.[41] According to senior ICE officials responsible for the Angel Watch program, the additional information USNCB collects and provides to its counterparts could also help support ICE's efforts. In particular, these officials stated that the relevant ICE attaché could share the additional information with that person's foreign counterpart to support efforts to deny entry or monitor activity of registered sex offenders. USNCB officials stated that it would be feasible to include Angel Watch program officials on the notifications USNCB sends to foreign counterparts.

Taking steps to ensure that USNCB and ICE have information on the same registered sex offenders traveling internationally—which could entail, for example, the two agencies copying one another on notifications to their foreign counterparts, or USNCB receiving information directly from NTC—could help ensure that USNCB and ICE are providing more comprehensive information on traveling registered sex offenders to their foreign counterparts to help inform public safety decisions.

Conclusions

Cases in which individuals who had previously been convicted of a sex offense in the United States subsequently traveled overseas to commit an offense against a child underscore the importance of sex offender registration and notification standards to help ensure public safety in the United States and abroad. Some of the limitations federal agencies have faced with regard to identifying registered sex offenders leaving and returning to the United States are expected to be addressed by the automated notification the FBI is currently developing. However, ICE has not requested to receive the automated notification, which may preclude it from identifying entire categories of sex offenders, such as those entering and returning to the United States via a land port of entry whose biographical information is queried. USNCB, U.S. Marshals, and ICE

---

[41]GAO-06-15.

have taken steps to coordinate their efforts to identify registered sex offenders traveling internationally, such as participating in the IWG and collocating staff. However, despite these efforts, these agencies still do not have access to all of the information on traveling registered sex offenders that they could potentially receive. Sharing additional information could help ensure that these agencies are providing more comprehensive information on traveling registered sex offenders to their foreign counterparts to help inform public safety decisions.

Recommendations for Executive Action

Given ICE's objective to target the transnational sexual exploitation of children, after the automated notification becomes operational, the Director of ICE should direct ICE Homeland Security Investigations officials to coordinate with FBI Criminal Justice Information Services officials to collect and analyze information that will enable ICE to determine if the benefits of receiving the automated notifications outweigh the costs. The type of information ICE may consider collecting as part of this analysis could include the number of notifications generated for sex offenders leaving the country via a land port of entry.

To ensure that USNCB and ICE are providing more comprehensive information to their respective foreign counterparts regarding registered sex offenders traveling internationally, we recommend that the Attorney General and the Secretary of Homeland Security take steps to help ensure that USNCB and ICE have information on the same number of registered sex offenders as well as the same level of detail on registered sex offenders traveling internationally. Such steps could include USNCB and ICE copying each other on their notifications to their foreign counterparts or USNCB receiving information directly from NTC.

Agency Comments and Our Evaluation

We provided a draft of this report for review and comment to DHS, DOJ, and State. We received written comments from DHS and USNCB, within DOJ, which are reproduced in full in appendices III and IV, respectively. DHS generally agreed with our recommendations in its comments, and USNCB agreed with our recommendations with additional observations. State did not provide written comments on the draft report. We also received technical comments from DHS and DOJ, which were incorporated throughout our report as appropriate.

In its written comments, USNCB agreed with our recommendation that the Attorney General and the Secretary of Homeland Security take steps to help ensure that USNCB and ICE have the same information on registered sex offenders traveling internationally. USNCB noted that it has already begun the process of establishing points of contact with the appropriate ICE personnel so that USNCB can include ICE in its dissemination of sex offender notifications. USNCB also identified additional actions which were beyond the scope of our review, such as the need for technical improvements to streamline data sharing and foreign notification processes. In addition, USNCB stated that there needs to be an impetus for all states to substantially implement the guidelines set forth by the SMART Office on traveling registered sex offenders. During the course of our review, officials from the SMART Office stated that they have taken some actions, such as conducting workshops and providing technical assistance, to encourage jurisdictions to implement the requirement for registered sex offenders to report international travel 21 days in advance of such travel.

DHS agreed with our recommendations that ICE should assess whether receiving the automated notifications would benefit their mission to target transnational sexual exploitation and that DOJ and DHS should take steps to ensure that USNCB and ICE have the same information on traveling registered sex offenders. However, in its letter, DHS questioned whether the automated notifications would be of use to the Angel Watch program because the timing of some of the notifications would not enable ICE to notify foreign officials in advance that a sex offender is traveling to their country, in which case the foreign officials could choose not to admit the offender. Nevertheless, in addition to admissibility decisions, foreign law enforcement officials with whom we spoke stated that they use the information they receive from ICE for multiple purposes, including determining how frequently the sex offender travels to that country, where the offender stays while in country, and where to direct their resources to monitor sex offenders.

DHS also raised concerns that given the hundreds of thousands of individuals leaving the United States via the southwest border on a daily basis, handling notifications on sex offenders leaving the country through this border may be untenable. However, it is uncertain how many of these individuals are sex offenders and how many of them will be queried by CBP when exiting the country. Therefore, it will be important for ICE to implement our recommendation so that once the automated notification process is underway, ICE can obtain the necessary information to determine if the number of notifications of sex offenders exiting the country through a land port of entry is manageable.

We are sending copies of this report to the appropriate congressional committees, the Attorney General, the Secretary of Homeland Security, the Secretary of State, and other interested parties. This report is also available at no charge on GAO's web site at http://www.gao.gov.

If you or your staff have any questions, please contact me at (202) 512-6510 or larencee@gao.gov. Contact points for our Offices of Congressional Relations and Public Affairs may be found on the last page of this report. Staff acknowledgments are provided in appendix V.

Eileen R. Larence
Director, Homeland Security and Justice Issues

Appendix I: Objectives, Scope, and Methodology

Since 2006, Congress has passed legislation and the Department of Justice (DOJ) has promulgated regulations to help ensure that federal, state, local, territorial, and tribal officials are aware of when registered sex offenders travel internationally. To determine the extent to which these officials have procedures in place to implement these requirements, we addressed the following questions:

(1) How and to what extent does the federal government determine whether registered sex offenders are leaving or returning to the United States?

(2) How and to what extent have federal agencies notified foreign officials about registered sex offenders traveling internationally?

To address both objectives, we identified legislation, regulations, and other guidance that directs federal agencies' efforts to identify registered sex offenders leaving or returning to the United States. Section 128 of the Sex Offender Registration and Notification Act of 2006 (SORNA), directs the Attorney General, in consultation with the Secretary of State and the Secretary of Homeland Security, to establish a system for informing domestic jurisdictions about persons entering the United States who are required to register under SORNA (referred to as registered sex offenders).[1] Further, SORNA makes it a federal crime for a sex offender required to register under SORNA to travel to foreign countries and knowingly fail to register or update a registration in the United States. Additionally, under DOJ guidance, jurisdictions are required to have registered sex offenders report international travel 21 days in advance and to submit information concerning such travel—such as expected itinerary, departure and return dates, and means and purpose of travel—to the appropriate federal agencies.

In order to assess how federal agencies obtain information on registered sex offenders leaving and returning to the United States, we obtained documentation from and interviewed members of the International Tracking of Sex Offenders Working Group (IWG), which is composed of

---

[1] For this report, jurisdictions refer to U.S. states, the District of Columbia, and the 5 U.S. territories. For the purpose of this report, we only included U.S. persons (i.e., U.S. citizens or lawful permanent residents) and foreign nationals who were registered as sex offenders in the United States at the time of their travel outside of or back to the United States. We did not include U.S. persons or foreign nationals who are not already registered as sex offenders in the United States, such as those who committed sex offenses abroad and may have to register under SORNA upon their return to the United States.

representatives from various components within DOJ, the Department of
Homeland Security (DHS), the Department of State (State), and the
Department of Defense (DOD). The IWG was tasked with developing
mechanisms to comply with statutory and regulatory requirements for
identifying registered sex offenders leaving and returning to the United
States. We reviewed the IWG's proposals for such mechanisms, which
were documented in a white paper prepared by the IWG in December
2010. [2] We then interviewed officials from three of the federal
departments represented on the IWG to obtain information on the
mechanisms by which they identify registered sex offenders leaving and
returning to the country, any limitations of these mechanisms, and what
steps could be taken to address these limitations. Those agencies are the
following:

- Department of Justice

  - Office of Sex Offender Sentencing, Monitoring, Apprehending,
    Registering, and Tracking (SMART Office)
  - Federal Bureau of Investigation (FBI)
  - United States Marshals Service (U.S. Marshals)
  - International Criminal Police Organization (INTERPOL)
    Washington – U.S. National Central Bureau (USNCB)

- Department of Homeland Security

  - U.S. Customs and Border Protection (CBP)
  - U.S. Immigration and Customs Enforcement (ICE)

- Department of State

  - Bureau of Consular Affairs (CA)
  - Bureau of Diplomatic Security (DS)

We excluded DOD from our review because under SORNA, the
departments responsible for dealing with registered sex offenders
traveling abroad were identified as DOJ, DHS, and State.

We also interviewed and surveyed relevant state, local, and territorial
officials to determine what role, if any, they play in informing the federal

---

[2]IWG, *International Tracking of Sex Offenders Working Group White Paper: An Interim
Report of the Collaborative Effort to Develop a System for Tracking Registered Sex
Offenders as They Depart and Enter the United States, as Required by 42 U.S.C. §16928*
(Washington, D.C.: December 2010).

government of registered sex offenders leaving the country, and how, if at
all they become aware of registered sex offenders returning to the
country, and how they use that information to help ensure public safety.
We first conducted a screening survey of officials from all 56
jurisdictions—the 50 states, the District of Columbia, and the 5 territories,
excluding tribal territories, that are eligible to implement SORNA.[3] We
contacted jurisdiction officials identified by the SMART Office as being
responsible for implementing SORNA in the jurisdictions to determine
whether they require registered sex offenders to provide advance notice
of international travel and whether they share information with relevant
federal agencies on registered sex offenders leaving or returning to the
country. These officials included representatives of state police
departments or attorney general offices. We pretested the survey with 2
jurisdictions, distributed the survey by e-mail, and received responses
from all 56 jurisdictions. Subsequently, of those jurisdictions that
responded that they require sex offenders to provide advance notice of
international travel, we selected 4 jurisdictions—Maryland, Florida,
Michigan, and Arizona—to conduct site visits and 1 jurisdiction (New
Mexico) to conduct interviews.[4] During the site visits we obtained
additional information on how they implemented and enforced the
requirement and shared information with relevant federal agencies. We
chose these jurisdictions based on (1) variation in the extent of
international travel from the jurisdiction; (2) percentage of the population
that is composed of sex offenders; and (3) whether the state has land and
sea ports of entry, in addition to airports, to cover the various modes by
which sex offenders could enter and leave the country.[5] During the site

---

[3]For this report, the 5 territories include: American Samoa, Commonwealth of the
Northern Mariana Islands, Guam, Puerto Rico, and the U.S. Virgin Islands. We did not
include federally-recognized Indian tribes eligible under SORNA because we will analyze
tribal jurisdictions' efforts to implement SORNA and identify registered sex offenders
leaving and returning to the United States in a separate review.

[4]During our site visit to Arizona, the Arizona agency officials responsible for sex offender
registration clarified that the State of Arizona does not require sex offenders to provide
advance notice of their international travel unless the sex offenders are planning to
permanently reside abroad. Consequently, to maintain consistency with our selection
criteria, we selected the next state jurisdiction that matched our selection criteria for site
visits—New Mexico. State officials in New Mexico did not respond to our request to meet
with them; however, we were able to conduct telephone interviews with relevant CBP and
U.S. Marshals officials in this state.

[5]Ports of entry—such as air, sea, or land ports of entry—are government-designated
locations where CBP inspects persons and goods to determine whether they may be
lawfully admitted or entered into the country.

visits, we met with officials from the following federal, state, and local law
enforcement agencies: U.S. Marshals, ICE, and CBP (at air, land, and
sea ports of entry), state agencies responsible for maintaining the state
sex offender registry, and local law enforcement agencies responsible for
registering and monitoring sex offenders. During the site visits, we
determined what actions were taken by state jurisdictions after the federal
government informed them of sex offenders returning to their jurisdiction,
particularly if the jurisdiction was not aware that the individual had left the
country. Furthermore, we gathered information from jurisdictions on any
actions that can be taken to improve their efforts to identify registered sex
offenders leaving or returning to the United States. While the perspectives
from the officials we interviewed during site visits cannot be generalized
to all jurisdictions, they provided valuable insights about registered sex
offenders traveling internationally.

We also developed and administered a second survey of the same
officials from the 56 jurisdictions to obtain more detailed information on
the extent to which jurisdictions implement the 21-day advance notice
requirement and inform federal agencies of registered sex offenders
leaving the country. The survey also included questions related to
jurisdictions' perspectives on any challenges or improvements needed
regarding receiving or providing information about sex offenders leaving
or returning to the United States, in addition to other issues related to the
implementation of SORNA. To develop this survey, we designed draft
questionnaires in close collaboration with a GAO social science survey
specialist and conducted pretests with 4 jurisdictions to help further refine
our questions, develop new questions, clarify any ambiguous portions of
the survey, and identify any potentially biased questions. Log-in
information for the web-based survey was e-mailed to all participants, and
we sent two follow-up e-mail messages to all nonrespondents and
contacted the remaining nonrespondents by telephone. We received
responses from 52 out of 56 jurisdictions.[6]

Additionally, during our interviews with the IWG agencies, we asked
whether any of these agencies use the information they obtain on
registered sex offenders leaving and returning to the country to help

---

[6]We did not receive survey responses from the following jurisdictions: American Samoa,
New Hampshire, Oregon, and Washington. For further details on the web survey,
GAO-13-211 and for the e-supplement containing the questions and results of the web
survey see GAO-13-234SP.

ensure public safety. For the three agencies identified as having
responsibility for taking action based this information—U.S. Marshals,
ICE, and USNCB, we obtained and analyzed data on the number of
registered sex offenders they received from August 1 through September
30, 2012 of registered sex offenders traveling internationally. We chose
this time period because we wanted to assess the effectiveness of a
process the U.S. Marshals instituted in August 2012 for sharing
information with USNCB on registered sex offenders traveling outside of
the United States. We then asked USNCB and ICE to provide us with the
notifications they sent to foreign officials about the registered sex
offenders who traveled outside of the United States for the same time
period. We also analyzed the data to determine the extent to which there
was any fragmentation (i.e. circumstances in which more than one federal
agency is involved in the same broad area of national interest) or
duplication (i.e. two or more agencies or programs are engaged in the
same activities or provide the same services to the same beneficiaries)
with regard to the notices. Specifically, we analyzed and compared the
data provided by U.S. Marshals, ICE and USNCB to determine the extent
to which the information these agencies had on sex offenders who
planned to travel outside of the country was similar or different. We also
assessed the similarities and differences in the notifications sent by
USNCB and ICE to their foreign counterparts. We assessed the reliability
of the data the agencies provided by questioning knowledgeable agency
officials and reviewing the data for obvious errors and anomalies. We
determined that the data were sufficiently reliable for our purposes.

Furthermore, we contacted federal and foreign officials in select countries
to obtain information on how they learn of registered sex offenders
traveling from the United States to the countries in which they are located;
how, if at all, they use this information to help ensure public safety; and
any limitations or benefits of receiving this information. The countries we
selected are Australia, Canada, Mexico, the Philippines, Thailand, and
the United Kingdom. We selected Mexico, the Philippines, and Thailand
because, on the basis of data we obtained from ICE, these are among the
countries most frequented by child sex tourists—that is, individuals who
travel to another country for the purpose of engaging in inappropriate
sexual activity with a child. We selected Australia, Canada, and the
United Kingdom because they are known to have national sex offender
registries, similar to those of the United States, and have expressed an
interest in receiving information from the U.S. government on sex
offenders traveling to their countries. For each of these countries, we
reached out to the ICE attachés stationed in country as well as a
representative from the country's national law enforcement agency. The

perspectives of these officials are not representative, but provide valuable insights.

We conducted this performance audit from January 2012 to February 2013 in accordance with generally accepted government auditing standards. Those standards require that we plan and perform the audit to obtain sufficient, appropriate evidence to provide a reasonable basis for our analysis based on our audit objectives. We believe that the evidence obtained provides a reasonable basis for our analysis based on our audit objectives.

Appendix II: Registered Sex Offenders Traveling Internationally Who Were Refused Entry by Foreign Countries

CBP's National Targeting Center (NTC) reviews air and sea passenger data to identify registered sex offenders who plan to travel internationally. NTC shares this information with the U.S. Marshals and ICE. The U.S. Marshals then refers these travelers to USNCB, and USNCB sends notifications to its counterparts via INTERPOL to foreign countries so that these countries can take action they deem appropriate to help ensure public safety, such as refusing entry. Figure 3 shows, according to NTC, how many registered sex offenders NTC identified and referred to USNCB (through the U.S. Marshals) who were ultimately refused entry by the foreign country during fiscal year 2012.

Figure 3: Number of Registered Sex Offenders Referred by the National Targeting Center (NTC) to the U.S. Marshals and U.S. Immigration and Customs Enforcement (ICE), and Number Refused Entry by Foreign Destination Country, October 1, 2011, to September 27, 2012

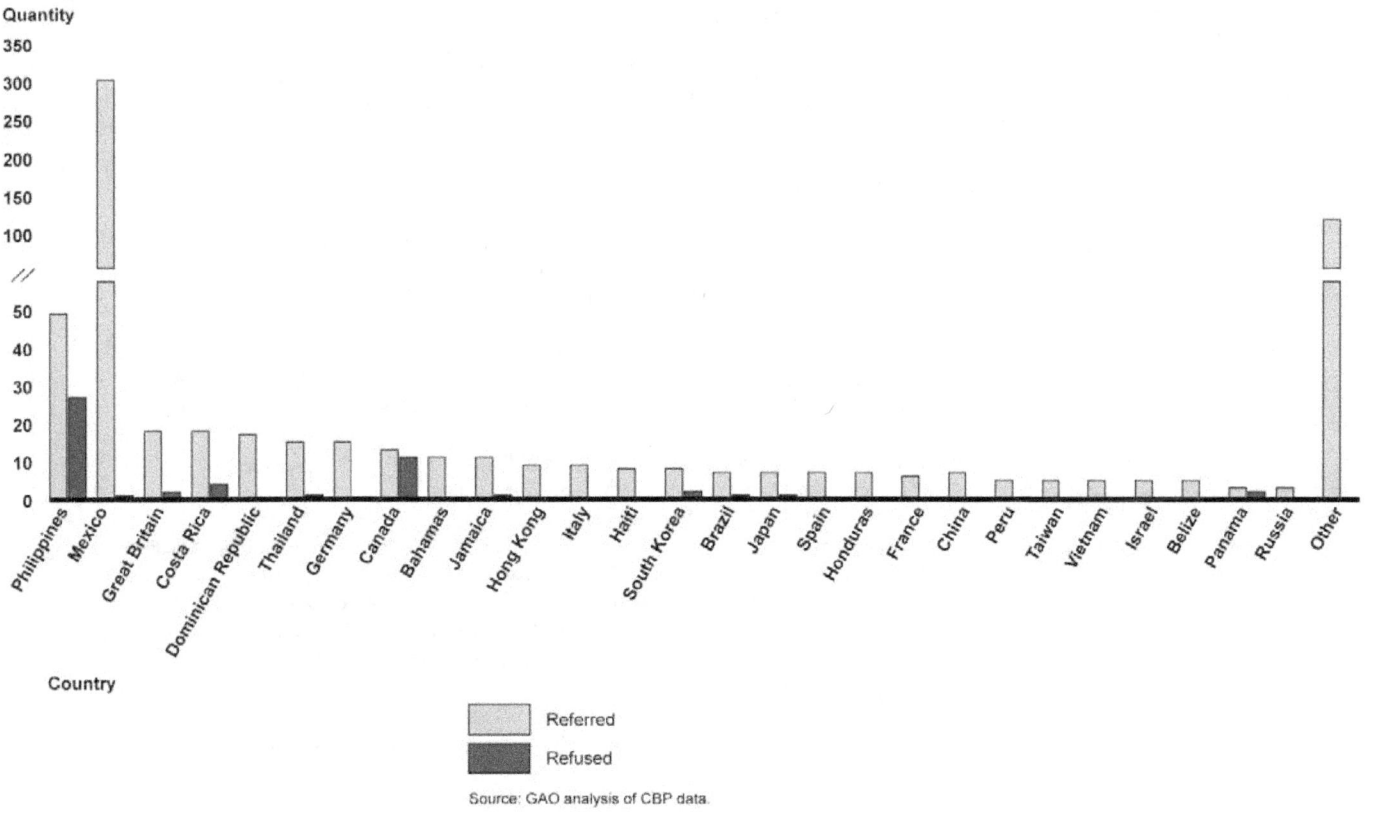

Source: GAO analysis of CBP data.

Appendix III: Comments from the Department of Homeland Security

U.S. Department of Homeland Security
Washington, DC 20528

Homeland Security

February 8, 2013

Eileen R. Larence
Director, Homeland Security and Justice Issues
U.S. Government Accountability Office
441 G Street, NW
Washington, DC 20548

Re: Draft Report, GAO-13-200, "REGISTERED SEX OFFENDERS: Sharing More
Information Will Enable Agencies to Improve Notifications of Sex Offenders'
International Travel"

Dear Ms. Larence:

Thank you for the opportunity to review and comment of this draft report. The U.S. Department
of Homeland Security (DHS) appreciates the U.S. Government and Accountability Office's
(GAO's) work in planning and conducting its review and issuing this report.

The Department is pleased to note GAO's recognition of the positive work U.S. Immigration and
Customs Enforcement (ICE's) is doing in conjunction with foreign counterparts to help inform
public safety decisions when registered sex offenders are traveling outside the United States.

The draft report contained two recommendations directed to DHS, with which the
Department concurs. Specifically, GAO recommended that:

Recommendation 1: The Director of ICE should direct ICE HSI officials to coordinate with
FBI's CJIS officials to collect and analyze information that will enable ICE to determine if the
benefits of receiving alerts from the automated system outweigh the costs. The type of
information ICE may consider collecting as part of this analysis could include the number of
alerts the system generated for sex offenders leaving the country via a land port of entry.

Response: Concur. Once the automated system becomes fully operational, ICE will assess the
information that is being collected to determine its applicability to Operation Angel Watch.

ICE's role in combatting child exploitation is investigative in nature. As noted in the report, ICE
receives information from CBP's National Targeting Center (NTC) of child sex offenders who
are traveling to foreign countries. Operation Angel Watch is an information-sharing relationship
between NTC and ICE, where the focus is to identify and target individuals who have a criminal
history of sexual-related crimes against children by reviewing the passenger data for air and sea
travel. ICE then sends this information as a notification to its foreign counterparts to alert them
before the individual in question enters that country. This enables the foreign country to take
whatever steps it deems necessary.

Operation Angel Watch is not intended to provide reporting of child sex offenders who are
traveling through land ports. The purpose and utility of Operation Angel Watch is that it
provides foreign counterparts with the information prior to the individual's arrival into the
country. There is a built-in time component that is necessary to ensure the information delivered
can be of utility to the foreign counterpart. Because of this, ICE's foreign counterparts are able
to make a determination as to how they want to handle the individual. For example, the foreign
country may deny admittance or they may admit the individual into the country but monitor the
individual's movement.

With the current proposed Federal Bureau of Investigation (FBI) automated system, the
information regarding land border crossings would not be transmitted to countries in a timely
manner that would enable them to make informed decisions regarding the sex offender's entry
into the country. If the registered sex offender is exiting the United States, the automated
notification received by ICE would have to first be vetted to determine if the traveler's offense
was against a child. Once this vetting is completed, the information would then need to be
forwarded to the appropriate ICE Attaché office, which would then contact the relevant foreign
counterpart to convey the information for a foreign law enforcement officer to then make a
determination as to what response or action to take. All these steps would need to happen in the
relatively brief span of time it takes the child sex offender to pass through the land border port of
entry and present himself/herself to the foreign customs official. Along the Southwest Border
alone, there are hundreds of thousands of individuals traveling out of the United States on a daily
basis. From a practical and logistical standpoint, such a notification structure seems inherently
untenable.

While the current proposed FBI automated system would not be of utility to Operation Angel
Watch, ICE will continue its involvement with the International Tracking of Sex Offenders
Working Group to determine if the proposed automated system can be altered in a manner to
capture information that would fit into Operation Angel Watch's purpose and construct.

Recommendation 2: The Attorney General and the Secretary of Homeland Security takes steps
to help ensure that USNCB and ICE have information on the same number of registered sex
offenders traveling internationally. Such steps could include USNCB and ICE copying each

2

other on their notifications to their foreign counterparts or USNCB receiving information directly
from NTC.

Response: Concur. ICE believes that being added to the U.S. National Central Bureau's
(USNCB's) notifications would ensure that it obtains useful information that USNCB is
receiving from other information streams, and thus help further investigate efforts related to
traveling child sex offenders. This would assist in enhancing the information-sharing process,
and would be a positive step in ensuring that information the USNCB receives relating to
traveling sex offenders is also received by ICE.

ICE is committed to ensuring that all necessary and useful information regarding traveling
registered sex offenders is transmitted to all relevant law enforcement entities. Currently, ICE
copies the U.S. Marshals Service (USMS) and CBP on the notifications it sends to its foreign
counterparts. USNCB should receive these notifications from USMS. However, USNCB can
also request addition to CBP NTC's distribution list. By being on NTC's distribution list, this
will ensure that USNCB receives the same information from NTC as ICE receives.

Again, thank you for the opportunity to review and comment on this draft report. Technical
comments were previously provided under separate cover. We look forward to working with
you in the future.

Sincerely,

Jim H. Crumpacker
Director
Departmental GAO-OIG Liaison Office

3

Appendix IV: Comments from the Department of Justice

U.S. Department of Justice

INTERPOL Washington

U.S. National Central Bureau

Washington, DC 20530

1 February 2013

Eileen R. Larence
Director
Homeland Security and Justice
U.S. Government Accountability Office
441 G Street, NW
Washington, DC 20548

Dear Ms. Larence,

Thank you for the opportunity to review and comment on the final draft of the Government Accountability Office (GAO) report entitled "Sharing More Information Will Enable Federal Agencies to Improve Notifications of Sex Offenders' International Travel". This letter constitutes INTERPOL Washington's formal comments. I request that the GAO include this letter in the final report.

As recommended in the report, INTERPOL Washington has already begun the process of establishing points of contact with the appropriate ICE personnel for dissemination of the sex offender notification messages. We anticipate a smooth transition in adding our ICE colleagues into the process. Additionally, the National Targeting Center (NTC) through the U.S. Marshals Service is now providing INTERPOL Washington with additional information on non-compliant sex offenders who have not yet travelled. INTERPOL Washington will in turn notify our foreign counterparts of the impending travel.

While I view this recommendation as a step in the right direction, I am concerned that it doesn't fully address the specific issues involved. Technical improvements are needed to streamline the data sharing and foreign notification processes amongst all of the concerned agencies. Further, a method for data de-confliction must be established. In addition, in order to make this program successful there needs to be an impetus for all of the states to substantially implement the guidelines as set forth by the Office of Sex Offender Sentencing, Monitoring, Apprehending, Registering, and Tracking (SMART). Finally, standardizing reporting and requiring participation from all jurisdictions may require further legislative action.

Even in these times of severely restricted budgets, INTERPOL Washington considers this
program to be a priority. We will support the improvement of the processes to the fullest
extent our existing resources allow.

Sincerely,

Shawn A. Bray
Director

cc: Suzanne Johnson, Audit Liaison
U. S. Department of Justice

Appendix V: Contact and Staff Acknowledgments

GAO Contact	Eileen R. Larence, (202) 512-8777 or larencee@gao.gov
Acknowledgments	In addition to the contact named above, Kristy Brown, Assistant Director; Su Jin Yon, Analyst-in-Charge; and Alicia Loucks made significant contributions to the report. Other key contributors were Susan Baker, Gary Bianchi, Frances Cook, Anthony DeFrank, Heather Dunahoo, Michele Fejfar, Eric Hauswirth, Richard Eiserman, Lara Miklozek, Linda Miller, Anthony Moran, Sheena Smith, Julie Spetz, and John Vocino.

GAO's Mission	The Government Accountability Office, the audit, evaluation, and investigative arm of Congress, exists to support Congress in meeting its constitutional responsibilities and to help improve the performance and accountability of the federal government for the American people. GAO examines the use of public funds; evaluates federal programs and policies; and provides analyses, recommendations, and other assistance to help Congress make informed oversight, policy, and funding decisions. GAO's commitment to good government is reflected in its core values of accountability, integrity, and reliability.
Obtaining Copies of GAO Reports and Testimony	The fastest and easiest way to obtain copies of GAO documents at no cost is through GAO's website (http://www.gao.gov). Each weekday afternoon, GAO posts on its website newly released reports, testimony, and correspondence. To have GAO e-mail you a list of newly posted products, go to http://www.gao.gov and select "E-mail Updates."
Order by Phone	The price of each GAO publication reflects GAO's actual cost of production and distribution and depends on the number of pages in the publication and whether the publication is printed in color or black and white. Pricing and ordering information is posted on GAO's website, http://www.gao.gov/ordering.htm. Place orders by calling (202) 512-6000, toll free (866) 801-7077, or TDD (202) 512-2537. Orders may be paid for using American Express, Discover Card, MasterCard, Visa, check, or money order. Call for additional information.
Connect with GAO	Connect with GAO on Facebook, Flickr, Twitter, and YouTube. Subscribe to our RSS Feeds or E-mail Updates. Listen to our Podcasts. Visit GAO on the web at www.gao.gov.
To Report Fraud, Waste, and Abuse in Federal Programs	Contact: Website: http://www.gao.gov/fraudnet/fraudnet.htm E-mail: fraudnet@gao.gov Automated answering system: (800) 424-5454 or (202) 512-7470
Congressional Relations	Katherine Siggerud, Managing Director, siggerudk@gao.gov, (202) 512-4400, U.S. Government Accountability Office, 441 G Street NW, Room 7125, Washington, DC 20548
Public Affairs	Chuck Young, Managing Director, youngc1@gao.gov, (202) 512-4800 U.S. Government Accountability Office, 441 G Street NW, Room 7149 Washington, DC 20548